LAND THAT I LOVE
Regions of the United States

Niccole Bartley

PowerKiDS
press.
New York

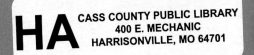

Published in 2015 by The Rosen Publishing Group, Inc.
29 East 21st Street, New York, NY 10010

First Edition

Editor: Joanne Randolph
Photo Research: Katie Stryker
Book Design: Colleen Bialecki

Photo Credits: Cover Semmick Photo/Shutterstock.com; p. 4 Richard Cavalleri/Shutterstock.com; pp. 5, 15 Todd Klassy/Shutterstock.com; p. 6 Eddie Brady/Lonely Planet Images/Getty Images; p. 7 George Catlin/The Bridgeman Art Library/Getty Images; p. 8 Jennifer Thermes/Photodisc/Getty Images; p. 9 MPI/Archive Photos/Getty Images; p. 10 UniversalImagesGroup/Getty Images; p. 11 Archive Holdings Inc/Archive Photos/Getty Images; p. 12 Stocktrek Images/Getty Images; p. 13 John_Brueske/iStock/Thinkstock; p. 14 Zack Frank/Shutterstock.com; p. 16 (bottom left) Henryk Sadura/iStock/Thinkstock; p. 16 (bottom right) Wallace Weeks/Shutterstock.com; p. 17 (top) Frontpage/Shutterstock.com; p. 17 (center) Richard Cummins/Lonely Planet Images/Getty Images; pp. 17 (bottom left), 23 spirit of america/Shutterstock.com; p. 17 (bottom right) Digital Vision/Photodisc/Thinkstock; p. 18 BuddikaS/Shutterstock.com; p. 19 Henk Bentlage/Shutterstock.com; p. 19 (bottom) Bonnie Taylor Barry/Shutterstock.com; p. 20 Bankerwin/iStock/Thinkstock; p. 21 (top) John Terence Turner/The Image Bank/Getty Images; p. 21 (bottom) MaxyM/Shutterstock.com; p. 22 (top) Esme/Shutterstock.com; p. 22 (bottom) Rudy Balasko/Shutterstock.com; p. 24 carroteater/Shutterstock.com; p. 25 (top) Critterbiz/Shutterstock.com; p. 26 Rick Gerharter/Lonely Planet Images/Getty Images; p. 27 Kim Karpeles/age fotostock/Getty Images; p. 28 Ryan/Beyer/Photographer's Choice/Getty Images; p. 29 Karen Desjardin/Flickr/Getty Images; p. 30 Karen Bleier/AFP/Getty Images.

Library of Congress Cataloging-in-Publication Data

Bartley, Niccole.
The Midwest / by Niccole Bartley. — First edition.
    pages cm. — (Land that I love: regions of the United States)
Includes index.
ISBN 978-1-4777-6865-5 (library binding) — ISBN 978-1-4777-6866-2 (paperback) —
ISBN 978-1-4777-6637-8 (6-pack)
1. Middle West—Juvenile literature. I. Title.
F351.B37 2015
977—dc23
                                    2014002935

Manufactured in the United States of America

CPSIA Compliance Information: Batch #WS14PK9: For Further Information contact Rosen Publishing, New York, New York at 1-800-237-9932

CONTENTS

WELCOME TO THE MIDWEST

Chicago is the largest midwestern city. It sits on Lake Michigan.

The Midwest is a region of the United States. It is made up of 12 states, which are generally divided into two areas. These areas are the Great Lakes states and the Great Plains states.

The Great Lakes states are bordered by Canada and the Great Lakes to the north. These states are Illinois, Indiana, Michigan, Ohio, Minnesota, and Wisconsin. The Great Lakes states have urban and industrialized areas. People who live there enjoy sailing, boating, camping, and hiking around the natural wilderness of the Great Lakes region.

The Great Plains states are Iowa, Kansas, Missouri, North Dakota, Nebraska, and South Dakota. Much of the Great Plains was once covered in prairie. The Great Plains region is a rural area known for ranching and agriculture.

When people think of the Midwest, they often think of the Great Plains. Big, open grasslands like this used to cover much of the Midwest.

Humans first came to live in the Midwest about 10,000 to 12,000 years ago. Over 1,000 years ago, a mound-building culture developed along the Mississippi River. The largest-known collection of the mounds built by these people is found in Illinois and Iowa.

After the 1500s, the main American Indian groups living in the Great Lakes region were the Hurons, Ottawas, Chippewas, and Winnebagos. They lived in **wigwams**, hunted buffalo on the prairies, and fished in the Great Lakes.

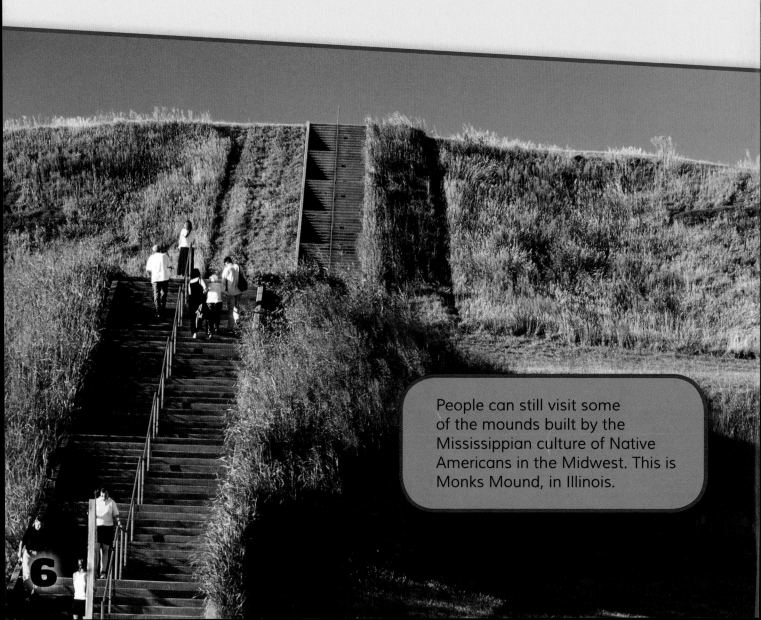

People can still visit some of the mounds built by the Mississippian culture of Native Americans in the Midwest. This is Monks Mound, in Illinois.

George Catlin, an American painter who specialized in painting Native Americans, made this painting of a buffalo hunt on the Great Plains in 1832. Native Americans killed only the buffalo that they needed to survive.

The Native Americans living in the Great Plains region followed the **migration** of the American bison, or buffalo, each year. They lived in teepees, rode horses, and hunted on the prairies.

WRITE ABOUT IT!

The Plains Indians counted on the buffalo for food, clothing, tools, and shelter. They wasted nothing. They had great respect for the buffalo and had many ceremonies honoring these great animals, which provided their means for living. Imagine you are a young Plains Indian and write a poem thanking the buffalo for everything it has done for your family. Do some research first to find out the ways in which the Plains Indians used the buffalo.

The first European to visit the Midwest was Frenchman Jacques Cartier. He **explored** the Saint Lawrence River region in 1534 and claimed the area for France.

In 1673, Frenchmen Louis Joliet and Jacques Marquette traveled by canoe from Quebec down the Mississippi River, proving it was possible to reach the Gulf of Mexico. After their trip, French settlers established fur-trading posts and missions in the Great Lakes region and along the Mississippi River. The area was called the Louisiana Territory.

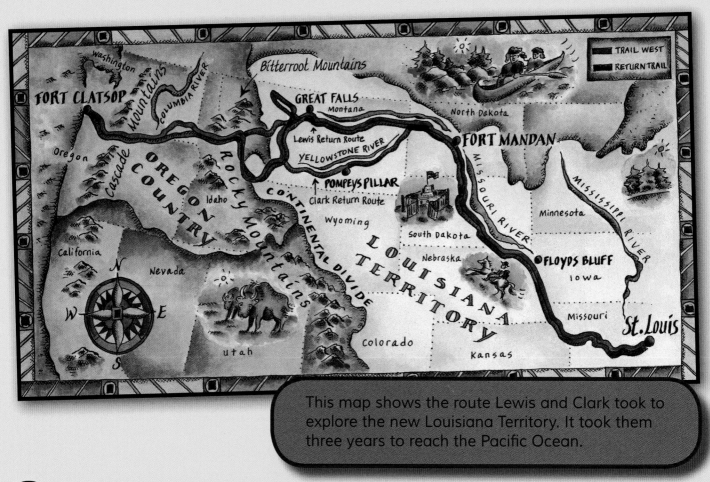

This map shows the route Lewis and Clark took to explore the new Louisiana Territory. It took them three years to reach the Pacific Ocean.

Lewis and Clark followed the Missouri River from St. Louis, Missouri, through the Great Plains of Iowa, Nebraska, and North Dakota. They made maps and drawings and met with Native Americans along the way.

In 1803, French leader Napoleon Bonaparte sold the Louisiana Territory to the United States in the **Louisiana Purchase**. In 1804, President Thomas Jefferson sent explorers Meriwether Lewis and William Clark to explore the land.

During the mid-1800s, the issue of slavery was causing the United States a lot of political trouble. Many states felt that slavery should be **abolished**. Many Southern states relied on slaves to run their large farms and threatened to **secede** if slavery was not allowed.

More than 100,000 slaves escaped to freedom in the North via the Underground Railroad between 1850 and 1860.

Chicago hosted a world's fair in 1893 that was open for six months. Forty-six nations were represented, and more than 27 million people visited the fair. This electric generator was just one of the exhibits at the fair.

The Midwest was the first large region to **prohibit** slavery. In 1821, though, Missouri was admitted to the Union as a slave state. In 1854, Kansas was officially opened as a territory for settlement. People began fighting over whether it should enter the Union as a free or slave state. The fighting was so violent that the events became known as Bleeding Kansas. In 1861, Kansas was admitted to the Union as a free state. The Civil War began three months later.

THE UNDERGROUND RAILROAD

Midwesterners along the Ohio River helped slaves go from the South to freedom on the Underground Railroad. This was a series of safe houses, which escaped slaves visited on their trip north.

GREAT LAKES

One of the defining geographic features of the Midwest are the Great Lakes. The five Great Lakes are Lake Superior, Lake Michigan, Lake Huron, Lake Erie, and Lake Ontario.

Minnesota, Wisconsin, Michigan, Illinois, Indiana, and Ohio border the lakes. Most of the large cities in the Midwest are located on the lakes, including Chicago, Detroit, Cleveland, Milwaukee, and Grand Rapids.

The Great Lakes are the largest freshwater system in the world. They cover 94,250 square miles (244,106 sq km). Lake Superior is the largest lake in the world.

LAKE SUPERIOR

LAKE HURON

LAKE ONTARIO

LAKE MICHIGAN

LAKE ERIE

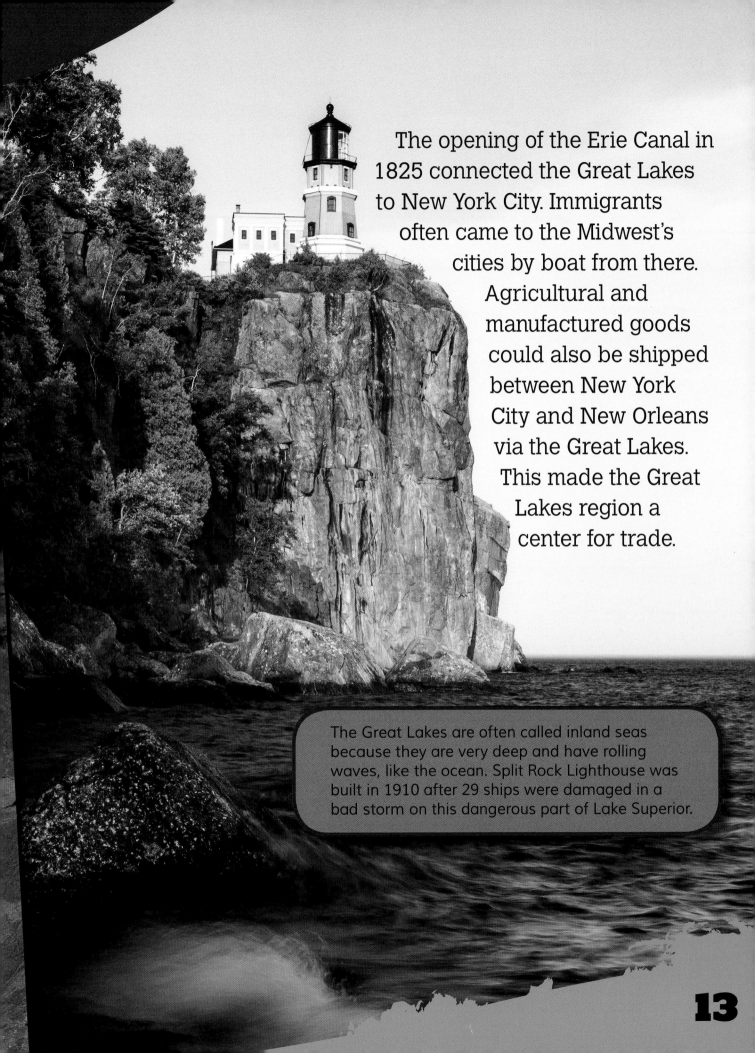

The opening of the Erie Canal in 1825 connected the Great Lakes to New York City. Immigrants often came to the Midwest's cities by boat from there. Agricultural and manufactured goods could also be shipped between New York City and New Orleans via the Great Lakes. This made the Great Lakes region a center for trade.

The Great Lakes are often called inland seas because they are very deep and have rolling waves, like the ocean. Split Rock Lighthouse was built in 1910 after 29 ships were damaged in a bad storm on this dangerous part of Lake Superior.

The Great Plains region is made up of wide-open, flat land. The Great Plains are located west of the Mississippi River and east of the Rocky Mountains. There are six midwestern states that lie in the Great Plains. They are Kansas, Nebraska, North Dakota, South Dakota, Iowa, and Missouri. These states are more rural than the rest of the Midwest.

The Great Plains are known for their wide-open expanses with few trees and only a few rolling hills.

Much of the Great Plains is now used to grow cereal grains, such as wheat.

The plains were once covered in prairies and herds of American bison. Now most of the land is used for wheat farming and ranching.

The Great Plains states have very cold and harsh winters. The summers are hot and humid. It is very windy and dust storms are common.

TORNADO ALLEY

Tornado Alley is a term for the area of the United States where tornadoes are most frequent. A tornado is a spinning funnel of air that touches the ground. Tornadoes are also called twisters or cyclones. They often destroy buildings, cars, and trees. All of the states in the Midwest have tornadoes, but they are most common in Kansas and Nebraska.

THE MIDWEST

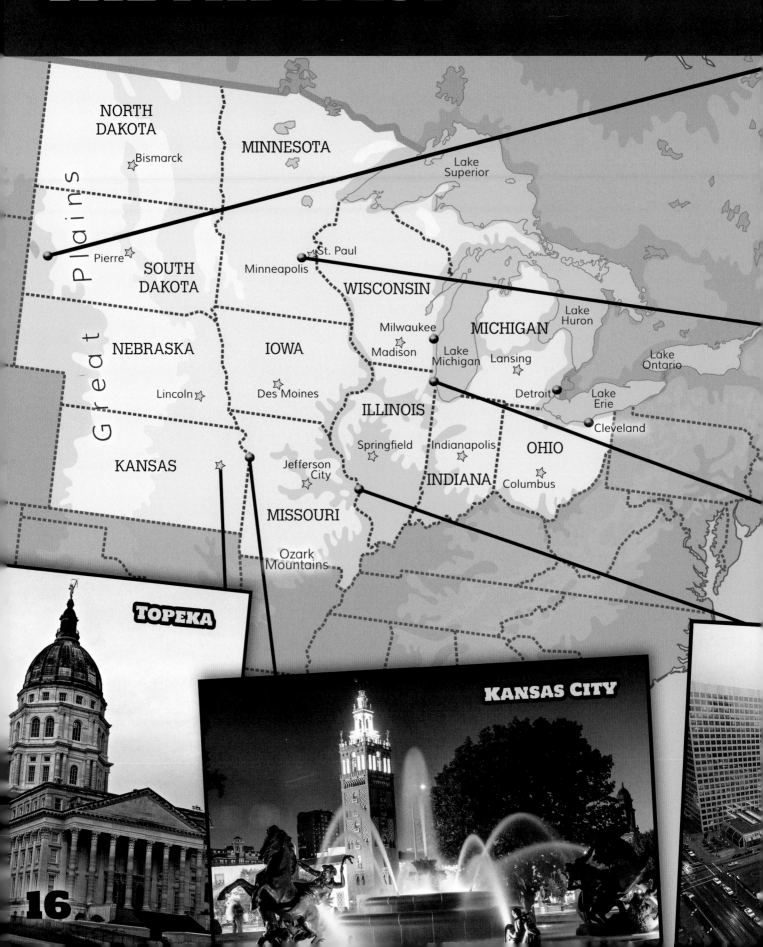

NORTH DAKOTA

Bismarck ☆

MINNESOTA

Lake Superior

Great Plains

Pierre ☆

SOUTH DAKOTA

St. Paul ●

Minneapolis ●

WISCONSIN

NEBRASKA

IOWA

Milwaukee ☆

Madison

Lake Michigan

MICHIGAN

Lake Huron

Lansing ☆

Lake Ontario

Lincoln ☆

Des Moines ☆

ILLINOIS

Detroit ●

Lake Erie

Cleveland ●

KANSAS ☆

Springfield ☆

Indianapolis ☆

OHIO

Columbus ☆

Jefferson City ☆

INDIANA

MISSOURI

Ozark Mountains

TOPEKA

KANSAS CITY

MOUNT RUSHMORE

MILL CITY MUSEUM

KEY

✦ State capital

● City or point of interest

Body of water

Mountain

CHICAGO

ST. LOUIS

PLANTS AND ANIMALS OF THE MIDWEST

The plains are known for their grasses and wildflowers. The areas around the Great Lakes have more lush vegetation, though.

In the early 1800s, the Midwest was covered with a sea of grass and wildflowers. This huge prairie was full of elks, antelope, deer, bison, and prairie dogs. Wolves and cougars followed the herds of bison.

Less than two percent of the prairie remains today. It was turned into farms and cities. Many prairie animals are gone from the Midwest forever. Smaller animals such as birds, coyotes, foxes, deer, badgers, gophers, groundhogs, and squirrels still live in the Midwest, though.

Prairie dogs live in the remaining grasslands of the Great Plains. These animals were once plentiful, but their numbers have gone down 98 percent in the past century.

The Great Lakes region of the Midwest is home to many shoreline plants, birds, and fish. Many migrating birds, including bald eagles, herons, loons, and piping plovers, come to the Great Lakes region each year.

The bobwhite quail likes to live in grass-filled open spaces, which makes the Great Plains a perfect place for them. Their numbers have decreased as grassland is replaced with farmland, cities, and towns.

NATURAL RESOURCES AND INDUSTRY

The Midwest's **fertile** soil made agriculture the main industry. It is home to the nation's biggest farms and cattle operations. Cereal crops, such as corn, oats, and wheat, are produced there. The many waterways and ports in the Midwest also caused a boom in the shipping, transportation, and manufacturing industries.

Huge fields of corn or wheat are common sights in the Midwest. The region has the nickname the nation's breadbasket because it grows many of the crops that feed the country.

Many important **inventions** were made in the Midwest. John Deere invented the steel plow. This allowed settlers to farm the deep, thick prairie soil. Henry Ford invented the movable assembly line for the mass production of automobiles. Detroit became the world's automotive center for a time.

The Midwest is known for being a leader in the manufacturing industry and especially for making cars.

The Midwest has more than 9,000 dairy farms, where cows are raised for their milk. One cow can provide around 44 servings of milk each day.

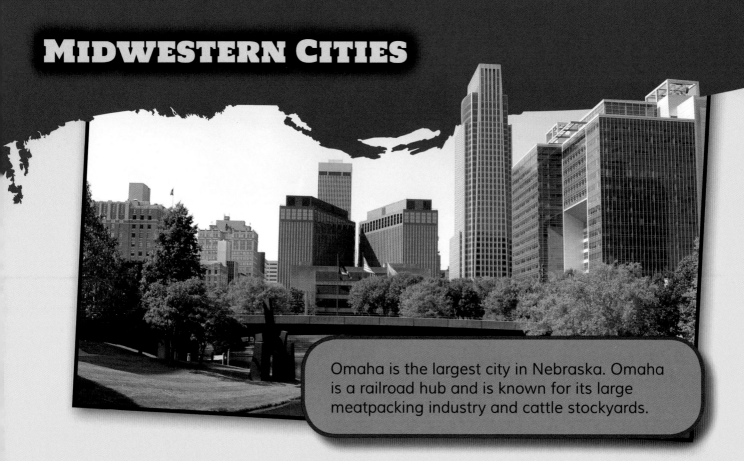

Omaha is the largest city in Nebraska. Omaha is a railroad hub and is known for its large meatpacking industry and cattle stockyards.

Chicago is the largest city in Illinois and the third-largest city in the country. It sits on the shores of Lake Michigan. In 1833, just 200 people lived in Chicago. Today there are 2.5 million people living there. In 1871, the Great Chicago Fire destroyed much of the city, and it had to be rebuilt. The world's first steel skyscraper was constructed in 1885 in Chicago.

Cincinnati is the third-largest city in Ohio. It was the first city founded after the American Revolution. It is famous for its chili and is home to many large corporations.

Detroit is the largest city in Michigan. Detroit has the nickname the Motor City because it was the headquarters of the American automobile industry.

Kansas City is the largest city in Missouri, though Jefferson City is the state's capital. Kansas City is famous for its jazz and blues music and Kansas City-style barbecue.

St. Louis is a port city in Missouri that sits on the Mississippi River. It is famous for its Gateway Arch, a 630-foot (192-m) memorial to westward expansion in the United States.

There is a lot to see and do in the Midwest. Chicago is the biggest city in the Midwest. The Navy Pier on Lake Michigan is a popular tourist stop there. It has shops, restaurants, and other fun places. The Field Museum is a famous natural-history museum in Chicago.

The Mill City Museum, in Minneapolis, Minnesota, is built inside the ruins of an old flour mill. Cleveland is home to the Rock and Roll Hall

Another midwestern landmark is the Indianapolis Motor Speedway, in Indianapolis, Indiana. It is home to the Indianapolis 500.

The presidents whose faces are carved into Mount Rushmore are George Washington, Thomas Jefferson, Theodore Roosevelt, and Abraham Lincoln. Not everyone was happy about the creation of this monument. The Black Hills, where it was carved, are sacred to the Sioux nation.

of Fame and Museum, and many people visit Kansas City to see its beautiful fountains and taste its famous barbecue.

One of the most impressive landmarks in the Midwest is Mount Rushmore, in South Dakota. Sculptures of the heads of four US presidents are carved into the mountain.

The Willis Tower, formerly known as the Sears Tower, is a famous landmark in Chicago. The Willis Tower is the tallest building in this photograph.

MIDWESTERN CULTURE

The American **pioneer** spirit shaped the Midwest in the 1800s. As people headed west to expand the United States and seek new opportunities, the agricultural wealth and access to major waterways made the Midwest an appealing place to settle.

In the late 1800s, the Mississippi River inspired two classic American books by Mark Twain. They are called *Life on the Mississippi* and *The Adventures of Huckleberry Finn*. Twain's tales describe life in the Midwest at that time.

Tourists and Missouri residents alike enjoy visiting the St. Louis Art Museum. This gallery in the museum showcases German painter Max Beckmann's work.

Midwesterners are praised as being open, friendly, and straightforward. Their politics tend to be conservative. Farmers and pioneers by ancestry, midwesterners have a shared belief in personal liberty and freedom. The Midwest is famous for the creation of the one-room public school and has strong state universities.

The midwestern accent is often called the standard American English pronunciation. Many national radio and television announcers have midwestern accents.

There are many professional sports teams in the Midwest. Here thousands of fans watch a Chicago Cubs game in the city's Wrigley Field.

Midwestern cuisine is traditional American home cooking. The region's farms produce much of the nation's vegetables, grains, and meats.

The cities and their immigrant communities have more diverse cuisines. Chicago is famous for its deep-dish pizza and for all-beef hot dogs served on poppy seed buns with mustard, relish, onions, and tomato. Leave off the ketchup! Cincinnati is known for its richly flavored chili, and Kansas City is known for its barbecue.

The Mississippi River plays a big part in midwestern culture. Not only do companies use it to ship goods, but people also enjoy boat rides on the river. This boat is heading toward Minneapolis, Minnesota.

There is a lot of natural beauty for people to enjoy in the Midwest. This man is camping in South Dakota's Badlands.

REGIONAL RECIPES:
BUILD A CHICAGO HOT DOG

INGREDIENTS
1 all-beef hot dog
1 poppy seed hot dog bun
1 tablespoon yellow mustard
1 tablespoon sweet green pickle relish

1 tablespoon chopped onion
4 tomato wedges
1 dill pickle spear
2 sport peppers
1 dash celery salt

DIRECTIONS
1. Bring a pot of water to boil. Reduce heat to low, place the hot dog in the water, and cook 5 minutes or until done. Remove the hot dog and set aside.
2. Place the hot dog in the bun. Pile on the toppings in this order: yellow mustard, sweet green pickle relish, onion, tomato wedges, pickle spear, sport peppers, and celery salt. The tomatoes should be nestled between the hot dog and the top of the bun. Place the pickle between the hot dog and the bottom of the bun. Don't even think about ketchup!

The Midwest is home to the Great Lakes and the Great Plains. Pioneers and **homesteaders** were drawn by these features to settle in the region in the late 1800s.

Today the Midwest is a transportation hub and a big food producer for the nation. It is often called America's heartland for these reasons and also because it is considered the best representation of American culture. Whether you are visiting one of the region's cities or enjoying the beauty of the Great Lakes, you will find a warm welcome in the Midwest.

When people think of America, they often picture the wide-open fields and farms of the midwestern plains states.

GLOSSARY

abolished (uh-BAH-lishd) Done away with.

explored (ek-SPLORD) Traveled over little-known land.

fertile (FER-tul) Good for making and growing things.

homesteaders (HOHM-steh-derz) People who settle on land granted by the government under the Homestead Act, which gave a 160-acre (65 ha) piece of public land to people willing to farm it.

inventions (in-VEN-shunz) New things made by people.

Louisiana Purchase (loo-ee-zee-AN-uh PUR-chus) Land that the United States bought from France in 1803.

migration (my-GRAY-shun) The movement of people or animals from one place to another.

pioneer (py-uh-NEER) One of the first people to settle in a new area.

prohibit (proh-HIH-bet) To stop from doing something.

secede (sih-SEED) To withdraw from a group or a country.

wigwams (WIG-wahmz) Domed Native American shelters.

INDEX

WEBSITES

Due to the changing nature of Internet links, PowerKids Press has developed an online list of websites related to the subject of this book. This site is updated regularly. Please use this link to access the list:

www.powerkidslinks.com/ltil/midw/